# THE OTHER
# **MIRROR**

## Michael Mc Afee

# THE OTHER MIRROR

"Mirror, Mirror on the wall, who's the fairest of them all?" Most of us have probably read the story of Snow White and are well aware of the magic mirror in the story. Mirrors are important in our lives. We have mirrors in our homes, mirrors in our cars, and mirrors in our work places; some women have mirrors in their purses. Yes, mirrors are all around us because they are very important. Mirrors have different jobs, too. We have rearview mirrors so that we can see what is behind us while driving. I saw a bicyclist that even had mirrors on his helmet. Even though it gave him a visual of everything around him, he looked absolutely hilarious; it was as though he had eyes in the back of his head.

Have you ever been in a house of mirrors at the carnival? Mirrors can be fun; some can make you look fat or skinny; some can make you look tall, short, oblong, or just plain strange.

I watched a television show the other day that depicted someone who had been injured and stranded on an island. He saw a plane flying overhead, but how was he going to get the attention of the pilot? His solution was that he pulled a small mirror out of a suitcase. He began using that mirror to try to reflect the sun's rays toward the plane. It did catch the pilot's eye, and a few hours later, the man was rescued.

Yes, mirrors have different uses, but the type of mirror that I am thinking about today is a vanity mirror. It used to be called a reflecting glass for it reflected to the person who stood in front of it —- his or her image. That is important. Who would want to go out to a very important meeting with toothpaste still covering their lips or a shirt that is buttoned wrong—or worse? We all use mirrors, and when we do not like what we see, we usually try to change the problem, not the mirror, for the mirror is just reflecting the image that is before it. The mirror is not usually the problem; in fact, it is helpful for it shows what is good and what is bad so that we can make any appropriate changes to avoid any kind of embarrassment.

Mirrors do not lie. They tell the absolute truth; they hide nothing. The only thing that made the mirror magical in the classic Snow White fairy-tale is that the mirror spoke. Otherwise, it did what all mirrors do: show the truth of what it's reflecting. Snow White's step-mother stood before the mirror every day because she knew that it told the truth. And every day she was ecstatic because it told her exactly what she wanted to hear, and it never lied to her. *"Mirror, Mirror on the wall, who's the fairest of them all?"* Every morning the mirror would speak frankly: *"You are, Oh Queen."* The mirror didn't lie; the mirror wasn't emotional; the mirror just spoke THE TRUTH- the way it was. The mirror didn't particularly like the queen but neither did it dislike her. There was no relationship there; thus, the mirror spoke only what it saw and wasn't bound either to hurt the queen or to encourage the queen. The mirror told the absolute truth. That was good enough for the queen. She loved being the most beautiful in the land and liked having it confirmed daily. That mirror brought her much happiness.

One day, the queen jumped out of bed, put on her clothes, did her make-up and stood in front of the mirror before going out for the day. Why should this day be any different? Surely, the mirror would reflect absolute beauty and state it as a matter of fact. Up to the mirror she walked, head held high. *"Mirror, Mirror on the wall, who's the fairest of them all?"* she asked. *"Snow White,"* said the mirror. The queen, face flushed with both embarrassment and anger, asked again, *"Mirror, Mirror on the wall, who's the fairest of them all!?"* The mirror did not change its mind, but spoke truthfully, *"Snow White."*

The queen must do something about this. Something had to be done. Notice what the queen did not do. She did not throw anything at the mirror, she did not destroy or damage the mirror, nor did she throw the mirror away. Why? Because The Step-Mother's problem was not the mirror. It did what it was supposed to do; the mirror told the truth. She did what we all try to do when the mirror tells us that we are not the best: she tried to correct the problem. Unlike us, though, she tried to be the fairest, not by exercising more, nor by trying something different with her hair. She didn't go out and buy new clothes. She didn't even schedule an appointment with the nearest plastic surgeon for a tummy tuck, Botox or a facelift. No, she didn't want to change anything about herself. Instead, She tried to kill the one who had become the fairest in the land. Yes, that's right. She planned to murder Snow White. Obviously it didn't work, and depending on what rendition of the story we have heard; the queen either died in quicksand running away from Snow White or later was judged for the attempted murder and punished. Either way, it didn't work out well for the queen, and while Snow White lived happily ever after, the wicked queen was cursed.

The Bible has a mirror quality to it. Most of us have heard this preached, and we usually use the scripture found in James 1:23-25 *For if any be a hearer of the Word, and not a doer, he is like unto a man beholding his natural face in a glass* (mirror). *For He beholdeth himself, and goeth his way and straightway forgetteth what manner of man he was. But whoso looketh into the perfect law of liberty, and continueth therein, he being not a forgetful hearer, but a doer of the work, this man shall be blessed in his deed.* The Bible does have a mirror quality to it and for those of us who read and/or study GOD'S written Word, we can attest to this fact. The Bible reveals who we really are. It shows us what we are doing right, what we are doing wrong, our attitudes and even our motivations. Who among us has not had an opinion that we really believed, just to read something in the Bible that contradicted that certain belief? Did we change the Bible? Of course not. The Bible is the inerrant Word of God. And as God doesn't change, neither does His Word. So we changed our opinion to reflect the truth. How many of us were really down on ourselves, just to read the Bible and be reminded how precious we are to God? Perhaps during our daily Bible reading, we repented of a sin that was revealed to us? See, the Bible is a mirror and so when we read it, if it tells us that we are doing well, that is encouraging. If it tells us that we have failed somewhere, that we have sin in our lives, we don't throw out the mirror, for the mirror tells the truth. We don't blame any-body for it. We see the problem and we make the appropriate changes (repent) so that we once again can be "the fairest in the land."

So we see that:

- ✓ Vanity mirrors (also known as a reflecting glass) are important instruments in our daily lives.
- ✓ Mirrors are not emotional. They do not care whether we feel good or bad about the reflection. Their job is only to reflect our image back to us in an honest fashion so that we can choose to make any appropriate changes before being seen by others.
- ✓ One lesson that we can learn from the classic Snow White fairytale is actually taught to us by the wicked Queen. Instead of correcting the problem within her-self, she tried to eliminate the greatness of Snow White. Oh, that people would learn that life isn't a competition; thus, it truly is ridiculous to compare ourselves with others.
- ✓ The Bible has a mirror quality to it. The Bible is GOD'S inerrant written Word. It

speaks honestly. It reveals things to us. We can refuse to read it, refuse to listen to it, even throw it out, or we can look at it and make any and all necessary corrections and be blessed.

Although the Bible is a mirror that reflects who we are and it doesn't lie to us, we want to discuss the "other mirror" that we have in our lives, and also reflects who we truly are. Neither does this mirror lie to us. Can you guess what that mirror is?

## Jesus Was Impressed

Mark 12:41-44 is an interesting passage of scripture. [You can also find the story in Luke 21:1-4]. Jesus was at the Temple and He sat over against the treasury. The treasury was a room where people came for the purpose of giving money. On the wall were 13 trumpet-shaped containers to hold the money that people gave. So imagine with me, Jesus is in this room and people were coming in and dropping money into the trumpet-shaped money containers, and there Jesus was -watching the people give money to the Temple. Was Jesus there by accident? No, for we know that Jesus always obeyed The Father. Thus, we know Jesus was there for a purpose; the question is this: What was the purpose of Jesus being in the treasury? The answer is very simple. Jesus was there in the treasury just to watch people give money to the Temple. As He is watching, He sees the rich cast in a lot of money. This would have been the day to give abundantly, after all God in the flesh was watching. Now, people weren't paying very much attention to Jesus; they were just going about their lives.

Then while Jesus is there, He sees a poor widow come into the treasury. She humbly walks into the Temple where the rich are giving funds, and she drops into the trumpet-looking bucket the only two coins that she had. Those two coins would be equivalent to two-fifths of a penny— Not two-fifths of a dollar, but rather two-fifths of a penny. She literally didn't have a penny to her name. Yet there she is in the treasury, in the House of the Lord, to give a gift that would not even come to one cent. Jesus watches this and with excitement He calls for His disciples to come in to see what He is looking at. The disciples come running in. Jesus says, *"See that woman over there? She gave more than everyone else that has come into this house today."*

*"Her, Lord?"* one probably asked. "Yes, yes, that's her!" Jesus probably declared. "Well, she looks poor," another might have said. *"How much could she have possibly given?"* *"Did she win the lottery and is stopping here before buying some new clothes,"* someone finally asked. *"No, no, no, she didn't win the lottery. She is poor, and she gave a total of two-fifths of a penny,"* Jesus probably exclaimed excitedly with a pleased look on his face.

Then Jesus states: *"Verily I say unto you, that this poor widow hath cast more in, than all they which have cast into the treasury.* Mark 12:44

Jesus' comments probably took the disciples by surprise. How could this woman who gave less than a penny possibly give more than anyone else that day? "Jesus, did you not see that man over there- he gave a thousand dollars," one of the disciples might have said. "That man over there gave five thousand dollars," someone else probably said. Jesus simply said as he looked at the poor widow woman, *"Verily I say unto you, that this poor widow hath cast more in, than all they which have cast into the treasury.* Mark 12:44

Obviously Jesus noticed something that no one else saw and this was about to be a powerful teaching moment for the disciples, and hopefully for us.

## Why all the Excitement over Two-Fifths of a Cent?

I have been thinking about this poor widow woman. Let's start by stating the obvious:

(1) This woman was a widow. She had been married before, though we do not know anything about her or her husband. We do not know what kind of life they lived, but we could probably ascertain that she is old. How long has her husband been dead, we do not know even that.

(2) This woman is poor. She is impoverished. She has nothing. She doesn't even have one penny to her name.

(3) This woman comes into the treasury. Everyone there had more money than she did; yet she was bold and not too intimidated to come into the Treasury to give her gift.

(4) Jesus sees this woman give her gift, and He even knows the exact amount she gave.

Several times, the scripture tells us that Jesus knew "their hearts." If Jesus knew the hearts of those that He was around, surely He would have known this poor widow woman's situation. Why didn't Jesus go running up to that woman and call her by name and then explain to her that God didn't need her money and that she ought to just keep it? In fact, He could have said, *"Here's a little extra just for coming in today."* Why didn't Jesus scold her and say, *"You know, that's why you're so poor; once you get a little bit, you bring it into The Temple. That's not economically wise."* Why didn't Jesus encourage her by stating that after He rose from the dead, she would no longer be required to tithe? Jesus didn't do any of that.

Instead Jesus watched this woman give all that she had. The Bible doesn't even suggest that

Jesus said anything to her. She didn't know Jesus was there, but He knew she was there. Jesus may not have spoken to her, but He surely talked about her. We do know that Jesus was impressed with her gift even more than everyone else's gifts that day. Why was Jesus so excited? What impressed Jesus? He said that she gave more than everyone else. Surely, that couldn't be right! She gave only two-fifths of a penny.

Has your child ever asked you for a penny or nickel to put in a gumball machine? You may have searched your pockets or your purse, just to come up empty. If they needed a dollar, you could have come up with it; but really, who carries change anymore? Most of us would not even bend down to pick up a penny if we saw one on the ground. Because we have determined that "it's just not worth bending down for." We do not see the value in a penny. I can imagine that no one else in the Treasury that day, even carried the coins that were so invaluable. But this is all the poor woman had. She gave less than a penny while everyone else was giving dollars. So how could this poor widow give more than the rich?

Jesus said: *For as they (the rich) did cast in of their abundance: but she of her want did cast in all that she had, even all her living.* Mark 12:44

So did she give more than everyone else? Not economically, but she gave a whole lot more. She gave her all. I believe that it was more her heart than her purse, that impressed Jesus. She may not have been able to give a lot from her purse but what she was able to give came from her heart. I believe this poor widow woman desired to be obedient to the Lord and also she wanted to be a part of God's plan.

## Did God Need Her Money?

Did God need her money? The better question may be does God need my money? The answer would be the same… NO, God doesn't need anyone's money.

(1) Logic tells us that God doesn't need our money. Think about it, God spoke the worlds into existence in which He essentially made something (the universe and all that is therein) out of nothing. He is God! He is not in need! The very fact that

He is God means that He can fulfill His own needs all by Himself. How did God survive before man? Just fine. He created us for his good pleasure not because he was impoverished and needed man to fulfill some economic need. He is God!

(2) The Bible tells us that God doesn't need our money. ***For every beast of the forest is mine, and the cattle upon a thousand hills. I know all the fowls of the mountains: and the wild beasts of the field are mine. If I were hungry, I would not tell thee: for the world is mine, and the fullness thereof*** (Psalms 50:10-12). God owns it all. What are we going to give Him that He doesn't already have? Man makes his money using God's resources: wind, water, oil, wood, etc.

One day tax collectors came up to Peter and asked him whether Jesus paid taxes or not (Matt. 17:24-27). Peter's answer to them was, *"Of course He does."* Later, Peter told Jesus that taxes needed to be paid. Jesus didn't "freak out." He didn't say, *"Oh, no, what are we going to do? We will end up being thrown into jail by the IRS.*" Although Jesus didn't have money at the time, He wasn't anxious. He knew that His father wasn't poor, so He told Peter to throw a hook into the sea and he would find in the mouth of the fish enough money to pay for His and Peter's taxes. (Matthew 17:24-27)

We now understand that God doesn't need anyone's money. He is more than capable of meeting His own needs. Think about this: we could not ask God to meet our needs if He could not meet His own needs. We pray knowing that God is more than capable of meeting our need, whatever that need may be. Throughout the Bible God has always provided for the needs of people. He would not be able to do so if He were poor or powerless.

Jesus illustrates God's capabilities to provide at one point, by sending out His disciples and telling them to leave their wallets home. Yes, God was sending His disciples all over Israel without any money, just the word that God would provide. I would have loved to hear the testimonies of Matthew, John, even Judas on how God provided for them financially. God isn't impoverished. HE

IS ALL in All. He proved that when He introduced himself to Moses by calling Himself, "I AM that I AM." God is self-sustaining. He has always been and always will be God!

Jesus' reaction to watching people give in the treasury shows us that God doesn't need our money. If He did, Jesus would have been excited about the rich people casting in money and would have ignored the two-fifths of a cent that the poor woman gave. Instead Jesus said that she gave more than the rest. The purpose of Jesus' statement was the rich gave out of their abundance; in other words, it wasn't much of a sacrifice. They probably didn't give much thought to it, despite the fact that they gave a lot of money. They didn't consider the influence that their money could make.

Let me give another illustration. Imagine that a church is trying to raise funds to help build an orphanage in Bolivia. Bill Gates is sitting in the pew, listening to the missionary speak about serving the children and how they are in desperate need to be loved and safe and that the missionary is trying to bring the Gospel to that nation. When the offering plate is passed, Gates gives a check for one million dollars. (In 2008 Mr. Gates was worth around 56 billion dollars.) On the other side of the church sits Shirley. Shirley is a widow who makes $10,000 a year on social security. Although she has rent to pay every month and many other bills, she has managed to save $1,000, which is in the bank. She also sat there and listened to the missionary. When the offering plate is passed, Shirley writes out a check for $1,000 and drops all her savings into that bucket. Who gave more in the offering? Obviously, Bill Gates did. No question about that. It is obvious that the missionary would buy much more and be able to help many more children with the $1,000,000 that Bill gave rather than with the $1,000 that Shirley gave. However, which one would God have said gave more?

The answer is the poor widow. How can that be? For a multi-billionaire, a million dollars doesn't mean a lot. Bill gave out of his abundance. There was no sacrifice; there may not have been much thought. On the other hand, that woman gave all of her savings.

That's the gist of what happened that day at the temple, maybe not to the extreme of my illustration, but everyone else just gave. It was good that they gave; maybe they heard the pastor say that they needed to pay an electric bill or that something needed to be fixed, or maybe that is just what they normally did. Whatever the reason they gave, they gave out of their abundance without much sacrifice.

This particular widow was altogether different. First of all, she didn't have money to give, not a lot at least. She couldn't just throw in a few bucks. She had to eat and she had to pay her rent. She didn't have an excess of money. Not only that, what good could her two-fifths of a cent be? How could that small amount influence anybody or contribute anything meaningful?

Maybe the money that she had came by accident? Money was scarce and she needed it. However it happened, she found herself that day with a couple of coins; although she had needs, she wanted to be part of something bigger than herself. She didn't have much to give, practically nothing really, but she wanted to be a partner with God's Kingdom. This was worship for her. She loved God and wanted to show him in a tangible way. She could have used the money to eat.

She gave instead to something bigger than her circumstances. God didn't need her money, but God accepted her gift. In fact, it was the only offering that day, that impressed Jesus and was the only contribution that made Jesus smile. Let us remember, God doesn't need our money.

## So Why Give?

If God doesn't need our money, then why should we give? We give as an act of worship.

We know that even before the Law, there were offerings, sacrifices and tithes. Cain and Abel knew that they were to give to God. How did they know? Moses had not received the Law yet. In fact, Moses wasn't even born yet to receive the Commandments of God. Yet in the fourth chapter of Genesis, we see Cain and Abel for the first time. Guess what they are doing? That's right, they are bringing an offering to God. This lets us know right up front that Cain and Abel both knew they were to give to God. How did they know that giving was a part of worship? The Bible doesn't say, but maybe their father, Adam, thought it was an important lesson for them to learn.

Cain was a farmer.

Abel was a shepherd.

One day, both Cain and Abel brought God an offering. They came to worship. Cain, because he was a farmer, brought vegetables and things he harvested. Abel, on the other hand, because he was a shepherd, brought lambs, the first born of his flocks. God looked upon both gifts that each had brought to The Lord. God accepted Abel's gift, but rejected Cain's gift (which led to the first murder).

First, I find it interesting that God watched them both give. Centuries later we would see Jesus in the treasury of The Temple, just to watch people give. I find this humorous; the Son (Jesus) is acting just like His father (God). But we also understand that God sees every gift and every act of worship. No gift or offering goes unnoticed.

Secondly, in both scenarios we see that one offering was elevated above the other. Abel's offering was elevated above Cain's and the poor widow woman's offering was elevated above everyone else's that day. However, God not only elevated Abel's offering. He also actually rejected Cain's.

Why didn't God accept both Cain and Abel's gifts? The offering that pleased God came from Abel. Remember, Abel gave to the Lord the first lambs of his flock. The offering that was rejected came from Cain. Cain also brought the work of his hands, which happened to be vegetables and that which he had harvested. So why was one offering pleasing to God and the other offensive?

The answer could lie in God's remarks to Cain. Remember that Cain was very upset that his offering to God was rejected. In fact, so upset that he ended up killing his own brother because Abel's gift was accepted and his wasn't. Cain was jealous of Abel. There is a great similarity between Cain and the wicked queen of the Snow White story. The queen came to the mirror and asked "Mirror, Mirror on the wall, who's the fairest of them all?" If you can imagine, Cain came to God and asked "God, God, whose offering will you accept?" The magic mirror states to the queen that Snow White had become the fairest in the land, while God stated that Abel's offering was better. Neither the queen nor Cain liked the answer that was given to them. The answers were truthful, but instead of self-reflection and self-improvement, they both sought to kill the object of their jealousy. Neither sought to change their lives but rather to blame someone else for their ugliness.

Yes, Cain kills his brother Abel because of jealousy. He killed Abel because Abel's gift was better, but Cain completely missed the point. God didn't choose Abel's gift over Cain's because Abel's gift was better. No, no, no. God wasn't comparing the two gifts. The Bible tells us: And The Lord had respect unto Abel and to his offering: ***But unto Cain and to his offering he had not respect*** (Gen.4:4b-5a).

In other words, God essentially state, "I loved Abel's gift, but yours was a disappointment."

This is very important to note. It wasn't that God simply liked Abel's offering better, but that Cain's offering was a disappointment. Essentially, God turned his nose up at Cain's offering. God hated Cain's offering, and that is why he rejected it. The reason why God loved one gift and hated the other wasn't because one was better. They both gave from the work of their hands. But they didn't both give with the same heart. Look at Genesis 4:4b-5a **And The Lord had respect**

**unto Abel and to his offering. But unto Cain and to his offering he had not respect.** God had respect first for Abel and then to his offering. God didn't respect Cain, thus he couldn't respect his offering either.

Cain was upset because his offering was rejected. But the reason why his offering was rejected was that the man was rejected. GOD was better than the magic mirror we had just talked about. The Mirror just told the queen that someone was better. GOD is trying to show Cain the error of his way and trying to get him to repent. Remember, God asked Cain, "Why are you so mad? If you do what is right, don't you think that you will be accepted?" (Genesis 4:6-7a) God wants to accept Cain, but Cain has to do what is right to be accepted. Cain's offering wasn't simply the problem. Cain's offering was a reflection of Cain's heart. All offerings are a reflection of one's heart.

## Is Tithing A Part of The Law?

Some may say that tithing was part of The Law and so we are not required to fulfill that anymore. This is an interesting argument. However, the first tithe was performed before Moses was even born or The Law written. That's right! Tithing preceded The Law.

Remember when Lot was captured in Genesis 14? At the time, Lot was living in a country called Sodom. Sodom was at war. Sodom lost that war and a country called Elam took spoils from Sodom, they also kidnapped Lot (Abraham's nephew) who was living in Sodom at the time. Abraham heard about his nephew's captivity and decided to rescue him. He took 318 men and went to war with Elam. Abraham won that battle and rescued his nephew. Abraham also took spoils from Elam, which happened to be the same spoils that they had taken from Sodom. Then Abraham met with the King of Sodom and gave back to him what his nation had lost. Abraham gave to the Priest of God a tithe as a gift of worship, probably thanking God that he had been with them and that Abraham and his men were successful. The point I am trying to make is that tithing was initiated before Moses was even born and a long time before The Law was ever written. To say that tithing is a part of The Law doesn't give the full picture because though tithing was incorporated into The Law, it was established long before The Law.

"Just because the tithe was before The Law doesn't mean we are to still tithe," someone might argue. I would have to agree with that argument. However, we read in Matthew 23:23: ***Woe unto you, scribes and Pharisees, hypocrites! For ye pay tithe of mint and anise and cumin, and have omitted the weightier matters of The Law, judgment, mercy, and faith: these ought ye to have done, and not to leave the other undone.*** This passage shows us how Jesus rebuked the Pharisees for their hypocrisy. Evidently, they were paying tithes but were not walking in good judgment, mercy and faith. Jesus tells them they should be doing both. Nowhere in the Bible can one find that God negated the tithe. Nowhere! God has never said in the Bible not to give. Why? Because tithing and giving is an act of worship.

## How Did Ebenezer Scrooge Change?

Yesterday, I was watching *The Christmas Carol.* Everyone will remember the major character of the story – Ebenezer Scrooge. Everyone will remember Scrooge's favorite reply to the greeting "Merry Christmas." He would always say in his grating voice "Bah humbug."

Ebenezer Scrooge was a wealthy, but miserable miser. He was a banker, who saw a lot of needy people. Scrooge thought it best that the world would rid themselves of the poor. One Christmas Eve, according to the Charles Dickens tale, Scrooge is visited by three ghosts (the ghost from Christmas past, the ghost from Christmas present, and the ghost from Christmas future). It is an interesting night for the old miser. During a night of fear and terror, Scrooge is forced to self-reflect and to see the destination of the road that he has walked for so many years. It is an eye opener to say the least.

When the final ghost leaves after showing Scrooge his tombstone, Scrooge finds himself in a place of repentance. Scrooge is transformed from an old stingy miser, to Mr. Ebenezer Scrooge, the philanthropist. He begins to give of what he has to those who just a few days earlier he had considered worthy of prison or worse. Mr. Scrooge no longer is symbolized by his name, but is now happy, living life to its fullest; in his trans-formation he becomes a giver. To watch Ebenezer at the end of the show, we see he has learned by experience that the scripture is right: ***It is more blessed to give than to receive*** (Acts 20:35b)

Many people who call themselves Christians are stingy, thus reflecting a Scrooge persona. However, God never called us to be Scrooges and selfish, but He has called us to be a blessing to others. One way we do that is by the tithe.

## So what is a Tithe?

A tithe, simply speaking, is a portion—10% to be exact. The Hebrew definition of tithe is *a tenth part or a setting aside a tenth.*[1] We have estab-lished already that God doesn't need our money; therefore, logic would tell us that God doesn't need our tithe. So why should we tithe? I like Deuteronomy 14:22-23, ***Thou shalt truly tithe all the increase of thy seed, that the field bringeth forth year by year. And thou shalt eat before the Lord thy God, in the place which he shall choose***

---

[1]  The Strongest Strongs Hebrew 4643

***to place his name there, the tithe of thy corn, of thy wine, and of thine oil, and the firstlings of thy herds and of thy flocks: <u>that thou mayest learn to fear the Lord thy God always</u>.*** This scripture is a great explanation to why we tithe. It's not that God needs what we have, but that we learn to trust the Lord our God always. It is an act of faith. Yes, tithing is faith in action and The Bible tells us that faith without works is dead (James 2:17). We can say all we want about trusting God, but tithing is actually putting our money where our mouths are. This scripture tells us that we show our trust in The Lord when we tithe. This is one reason why I believe tithing is not simply an Old Testament sacrament. For if the Old Testament tells us that we are to trust The Lord, how much more does The Bible tell us about trusting (or having faith in) God in the New Testament? Tithing is a faith issue, and Romans 1:17b tells us that ***"the just shall live by faith."*** That simply means that as Christians, we live by trusting God.

Going back to our text, the poor widow trusted The Lord and gave to God all that she had. She must have believed what King David said, "I have never seen the righteous forsaken nor his seed begging bread" (Psalm 37:25). Remember, the rich gave out of what they had- their abundance. It was not recorded whether they tithed or whether they just gave an offering. However, we do know that they had much more that they could have given. The offering they gave took very little consideration. On the other hand, this widow had to give much thought to her gift because, in order for her to give something, she would have to go without something else. This means that the very act of her giving anything would be a sacrifice. She didn't give out of her abundance, for she had nothing. She gave out of her need. This woman had needs. For her to give anything, one or more of her needs were not going to be met. She had to make a choice- give to God or try to meet one of her many needs. She chose to give. She gave of her tithes and her offerings; she gave to The Lord. She trusted The Lord; thus, she was obedient. Thus, she was faithful- all an act of love or worship.

Let's take another look at Deuteronomy 14: 23c, *"And the firstlings of thy herds and of thy flock."* This is what Abel gave in the book of Genesis. Some have suggested that the reason why God didn't accept Cain's offering was because it was the wrong gift. Some Biblical scholars have suggested that Cain should have taken his fruits and vegetables and sold them to buy a lamb to make the sacrifice that God wanted. However, what those who believe this idea fail to realize is that the problem wasn't with the gift itself (i.e. God liking meat better than vegetables) for Deuteronomy 14:22 said: ***Thou shalt truly tithe all the increase of thy seed, that the field bringeth forth year by year.*** So we see that Cain bringing the vegetables of the ground, which was the work of his hands, was not the problem. So what was the problem with Cain's offering that God hated it so much?

I believe the problem wasn't with Cain's offering at all, but rather Cain's heart. The Bible doesn't tell us specifically but here are a couple of options: (1) Cain did not tithe on his fruits and vegetables. He just did enough to make himself look good. Or (2) Cain gave a tithe, but it wasn't his first 10%, nor his best. He probably waited and gave to God the spoiled fruits and vegetables, those things he would have thrown out anyway. He probably kept the best for himself, and he didn't give to God first. The result? God did not have respect unto Cain and wasn't even appreciative of Cain's offering.

Now before we totally condemn Cain, let's spend a couple of minutes in his shoes. What did Cain have to do in order to give to God an offering? He had to literally take the fruits and vegetables that he grew, let's say 10%. God didn't come down and put them into a basket and take it up to Heaven with him and say, "Thanks Cain." The tithe or offering that Cain gave didn't even go into a bucket so that he could eventually see his offering at work as we do now: i.e., church buildings, paying a pastor's salary, hearing how our money helped someone, etc. No, no, no. Cain had to take the tithe and offerings and build a fire and burn it. Think about taking 10% of everything you own and burning it; <u>Could we really convince ourselves that we are giving it to God?</u> Most would see it as waste. Cain probably did also; thus he might have taken the worst instead of the best and may have even skimped on the amount. Some Bible teachers have foolishly stated that God didn't want fruits and vegetables; He wanted a lamb, and that Cain should have traded with his brother to give the appropriate offering. That is simply not true. For we see in Deuteronomy 14:22-23 **Thou shalt truly tithe all the increase of thy seed, that the field bringeth forth year by year. And thou shalt eat before The Lord thy God, in the place which he shall choose to place his name there, the tithe of thy corn, of thy wine, and of thine oil, and the firstlings of thy herds and of thy flocks: that thou mayest learn to fear the Lord thy God always.** So we see that Scripture teaches us that we are to tithe on everything, including the fruits and vegetables. We may be impressed that Cain gave to God in the first place, but though we are impressed with what we see, God doesn't simply look at the flesh as men do; But God looks on the heart. (1 Sam. 16:7)

Abel, on the other hand, brought his first lambs. Abel didn't go through his lambs and give God a three-legged one or a sickly one. No, Abel gave to God first. He had to burn his offering just as Cain had to. The difference was Abel wasn't trying to skimp on the gift to God. He knew that God owned everything, including what was in his

own hand and that if God wanted the first portion, it was God's.

The poor widow (in our text) also had the
same attitude as Abel. They both thanked God
and worshiped God and stated practically that
they trusted God. The result? God had respect
unto Abel's offering. Jesus had respect unto the
poor widow's offering. We can certainly ascertain that Cain's gift wasn't really an act of worship,
nor an act of true obedience, nor was he walking
in faith. His heart wasn't in it; thus, God could
not accept Cain or his offering. Abel, on the other
hand gave God the first and the best of what he
had. His heart was one of true worship, thanksgiving, obedience and faith: the result-God had
respect for Abel and his offering. What does your
offering reflect about you? When the offering
plate is being past are you just dropping a dollar
so it looks as though you are giving or are you
truly worshiping God with what you have?

## Does Hoarding = Theft ?

***Even from the days of your fathers ye are
gone away from mine ordinances, and have not***

*kept them. Return unto me, and I will return unto you, saith The LORD of hosts. But ye said, Wherein shall we return? Will a man rob God? Yet ye have robbed me. But ye say, Wherein have we robbed thee? In tithes and offerings. Ye are cursed with a curse: for ye have robbed me, even this whole nation. Bring ye all the tithes into the storehouse, that there may be meat in mine house, and prove me now herewith, saith The LORD of hosts, if I will not open you the windows of heaven, and pour you out a blessing, that there shall not be room enough to receive it. And I will rebuke the devourer for your sakes, and he shall not destroy the fruits of your ground; neither shall your vine cast her fruit before the time in the field, saith The LORD of hosts. And all nations shall call you blessed: for ye shall be a delightsome land, saith The LORD of hosts.* Malachi 3:7-12

God is upset with Israel, and is speaking to them through the prophet Malachi in this passage. God is upset with His own people because they have completely failed God and have walked away from God's ordinances. The Hebrew definition of ordinance is (1) responsibility (2) duty (3) service (4) requirement (5) obligation (6) guard (7) watch (8) what is cared for.[2]

They were neglecting their responsibility, their duty and their service. The Children of Israel were failing in their requirements. They were not doing what they were obligated to do. They were not guarding or watching over what was given into their hands for care. They were not being good stewards. I am sure that they were letting God down in other areas beside their finances, but their finances did play a part in their rebellion or their neglecting of their requirements. The Lord tells them if they return to him, he would return to them. But they simply ask, "Where are we to return to?" or "Where have we failed?" God starts his answer with a question: "Will a man rob God?" That makes me ask another question: is God capable of being a victim of theft? The answer may surprise you.

Yes, GOD can be robbed. If I gave my son $50 and told him to run to the store and buy some bread, milk, chicken, and carrots; but he returned with a hamburger, fries, soda (which he consumed

---

[2] The Strongest Strongs Hebrew 4931

on the way home) and a few rental DVD's, would anyone not agree that he had stolen my money for his own purposes? I entrusted him with a certain amount of money for a particular thing, and he did something else with the money. Parents sometimes chuckle and say, "I would not call that theft." Ok, I put money in the bank, and I go to draw the money out because I want to buy a house. The teller tells me that unfortunately the money has been spent on the bank owner's home instead. I would be furious. The banker is entrusted with <u>my</u> money to distribute, as I desire, not what he desires or what he thinks is right. It's my money.

We have already established the fact that God is the Creator, and we have established that God doesn't need our money. In fact, Psalms 24:1 says, ***The earth is The Lord's, and the fullness thereof: the world, and they that dwell therein!*** Simply speaking, everything is God's property; we really are only stewards. We are managers over God's properties for he owns it all and we own nothing. So in the book of Malachi, God calls the children of Israel-thieves, for they had a responsibility to do with God's property what He desired. Instead they did what they wanted or what they thought was right. God gave them 100% of what they had, and He required 10% to be given back to Him as a symbol of their obedience, their thanksgiving and their faith. They refused, but instead took God's money and consumed it for their own lusts; thus, they began to serve their money instead of God. Jesus would later tell us in Matthew 6:24 that you can't serve both money and God; you have to choose. They chose to love money. 1st Timothy 6:1(a) states: **For the love of money is the root of all evil.** Money can reveal a selfish heart. Yes, money is a mirror. It won't tell you what you want to hear; it will tell you the truth. What does your money say about you?

When I was a kid, a friend and I were discussing a rumor about a man who had the audacity to break into a church and take the offerings. Even as children, my friend and I thought that no matter how desperate someone became, he/she should never steal from God. Yet by withholding their tithes and offerings, Israel was robbing God. That was not a wise idea.

We have already established the fact that God can be robbed, but is it wise to rob God? Logic would tell us NO! Robbing God is definitely a bad idea. As my friend and I agreed, "There are some people that you don't tick off," and God would be in that category.

According to Malachi, because Israel robbed God, Israel became cursed. Interestingly, disobedient people will often blame bad luck or circumstances or anything else for their misfortune and that is exactly what Israel did. Yes, Israel became cursed. God never intended for Israel to be cursed; they were supposed to be blessed and thus be a blessing to the rest of the world. Yet there they were: they had received a curse, but instead of repenting, they continued to rob God. People, even in the church, are like this. People who are supposed to be blessed, so they can be a blessing to others are living with a curse because they have disobeyed. They will blame so many other reasons for their misfortune instead of repenting and doing what they ought to do. It's like the Snow White story, the mirror tells the queen that someone is better, but instead of working to better herself- she attempts to kill Snow White. Snow white was not her problem. She was her own problem. Or like

Cain hating Abel and blaming Abel for the lack of respect that God had for him. But Abel wasn't his problem, Cain was his own problem.

God finally called Israel on their disobedience and said, "Hey, you have a curse on you because you have robbed <u>me</u>." "But how have we robbed you, Lord?" they asked. God replied, "In tithes and offerings." Many people rob the church, which they attend. People will come into the church and participate in worship. They enjoy the pianos, the guitars, the band, the sound system, the singing, but refuse to give in the offering. It's like going to a concert and sneaking in the back door. That's called "theft." People will come in and hear a message that will change their lives, but they won't give. That's like going to a seminar and not paying the registration fee. People will come in and receive prayer, they partake of communion, they use the bathroom, they receive all the benefits that the church gives, but will not give in order for the church to continue to provide these benefits. That sounds like theft to me. Some of these same people become incensed by people living on the street asking for handouts, but they come into the church and won't pull their own weight. With all that being said, and being true, tithing isn't just for that purpose. It is an act of faith, an act of love and an act of obedience. It is worship.

### What Is The Difference Between Tithes and Offerings?

Remember, Israel received a curse because they robbed God. How did they rob God? The Bible tells us they robbed God by withholding the tithes and offerings. So what is the difference between the tithe and offerings? Remember, we learned the tithe is the first 10%. Yes, they were to give the first 10% of everything they owned to The Lord. That may seem like a lot to some, but I would like us to remember the perspective.

1. God owns it all.
2. He has blessed us with what we have. It is God who gives us the power to acquire wealth.

God gives us 100% of the blessing and asks us to give back to Him 10%. We keep 90% of the blessing. Why does He give us 100% and then ask for 10% back? He could have just as easily given us the sum total of the 90%, but instead He gives us the total 100% and asks that we give 10% back to Him.

We have already established that God doesn't need our money. If that is true, maybe there is another reason for giving? Maybe, just maybe He wants to see if we will, in fact, put Him first, by giving to Him first. Maybe He wants to test our faithfulness in Him and our obedience to Him. We will either do with His money what He wants (making us trustworthy) or we will hoard it unto ourselves, which would make us thieves. Obviously, if we are trustworthy, He can give us more; if not, we may lose what we have.

So what is the difference between tithes and offerings? The tithe is a set amount, and everyone can do this. 10% of zero is zero. 10% of a dime is 1 penny. 10% on one dollar is a dime. 10% of $10 is $1. 10% of $100 is $10. 10% of $1000 is $100 and so forth. So far we aren't even talking about much money. Yes, but then 1 million dollars PRODUCES 100 thousand dollars and so 1 billion dollars has to give 1 million dollars – that's a lot of money. It surely is a lot of money, but most of us don't have to worry about that much money. Not only that, can a millionaire afford to give $100,000 away and not miss it? Surely he or she can. Everyone, no matter how old or young, how rich or poor, can obey God in tithing because tithing is a percentage of one's income. That demonstrates the awesome nature of God; everyone is called to worship God, to obey God and have in faith in God.

So what are offerings? An offering is not a required percentage, but is given according to one's desire. Offerings are gifts above the tithe. When Moses was commanded to build the Tabernacle, which was the portable church that traveled with Moses and the children of Israel through their 40 years in the wilderness, he asked the children of Israel to bring offerings. Now Moses was specific in what he needed; material, perfume, wood, gems, rings, earrings, etc. The people believed that God had indeed told Moses to build the Tabernacle. They took the request of Moses and made it into a reality. They had a desire to help bring the will of God into fruition. People even melted their jewelry in order to supply the silver and gold that was needed. They believed this was a God thing, and they wanted to be a part of it. It is important to note that Moses did not command people to give, but they gave out of their desire to help. I don't know if everyone gave or not, but it wasn't a command. It was a free will offering. How much did the people give? They gave so much that Moses had to command the people to stop giving. He didn't command them to give, but had to command them to quit giving. Their desire was to help, and they were willing to put their money where their mouth was. They were willing to stand behind something that they thought was originated by God.

What a difference between the nation at the beginning of Exodus when they were willing to get behind a God idea in contrast to the time of Malachi when they became selfish and went from being givers to hoarders.

## What Are The Benefits of Tithing?

There are so many benefits to tithing because it is being obedient to God and living in faith. We already saw in Deuteronomy that tithing was trusting The Lord, but in Malachi the word is "Prove." God says, "Prove me to see if I..." In other words, "Go ahead and tithe and see if I will not perform for you." The following are the things that God said would happen:

## 1. You're Blessed; With Abundance

There are multitudes of scriptures that shows us the benefits or blessings that we receive when we obey God, just as there are multiple scriptures of curses that come upon us when we disobey God. One of the things that Malachi says is ***"I will open up the windows of Heaven and pour you out a blessing that you cannot contain it all."*** (Malachi 3:10c) Wow, what a promise! God would bless us so much that we could not contain it all. I am reminded of the scripture in Luke 6:38 where Jesus says "Give, and it shall be given unto you: good measure, pressed down, and shaken together, and running over, shall men give unto your bosom. For with the same measure that ye mete withal (give) it shall be measured to you again." Wow, that sounds like a blessing! Not only will it return unto me, but it will be heaping (good measure), pressed down (to make room for more), shaken together, (to make room for more), and then there's still not enough room in the container, so it is spilling over. We can't even contain it all.

## 2. You're Blessed; By The Rebuking Of The Devourer

*And I will rebuke the devourer for your sakes, and he shall not destroy the fruits of the ground.* (Malachi 3:11a) God, Himself, has promised that he would rebuke the devourer. Isn't that exciting? God is doing the rebuking of the devourer. What a promise!

One of the definitions of rebuke is prevent.

We know who God is speaking about when He uses the word "devourer." It is the devil himself. He is a thief; he is a destroyer. He eats things up, just so we can't have it. I wonder if some of our financial problems are an attack of the enemy. I am in no way saying that all of our financial problems are a spiritual battle, but have we ever prayed that God would perform a financial miracle for us? Of course, people believe that God can and will meet our financial needs. If God can give to us financial things and we consider that a blessing from The Father, why can't we also see that sometimes our financial problems are a result of the thief coming in and stealing. Let me say again, not all our financial problems are a result of the enemy coming in to steal. Very often, Satan doesn't have to steal money because most Christians are wasting their money and going into debt to fulfill the lusts of their flesh. Quite a few Christians don't need the enemy devouring their savings, for they refuse to save. They don't need the enemy to waste their money, for they are wasting their own money all by themselves. They destroy their own fields. They have no idea where their money has gone, for they haven't properly managed their money.

But this scripture lets us know that there is a devourer or destroyer trying to eat up the blessings in our lives. It's like a cared-for garden that encounters a rabbit. The rabbit comes in and begins to munch on the work of one's hands, thus taking away from us and our families. The enemy works the same way. He is trying to destroy the fruits of our ground, but God has promised to be there to prevent him from doing that. The result is a fresh garden of blessings. God prevents the devourer. That's a good promise. How blessed we would be if GOD prevents the devourer from stealing from our finances, and we begin to be responsible over our finances so that we no longer waste our money.

### 3. You're Blessed; Your Fruit Will Come To Fruition

*Neither shall your vine cast her fruit before the time in the field, saith The Lord of hosts.* (Malachi 3:11b) This may not always sound like a great promise because we are "now" people. We do not always like to be patient, but we want things done now. It would be great to sow now and to reap tomorrow. Unfortunately, it doesn't work that way. This scripture talks about the timing of The Lord and how the timing will be perfect. The promise of God is that our vine will not give forth her fruit before it is ready. It will come forth when it's perfect in size and taste. Sometimes we pick too early; it's not ripe and is good for nothing. Or it may taste fine, but had it been on the vine just another week, it would have been bigger or better. We're always looking at our field, and the temptation is to go and pick. God lets us know that his timing is perfect, and our vine will not even give forth her fruit until it's ready.

### 4. You're Blessed; All Nations Shall Call You Blessed

***And all nations shall call you blessed: for ye shall be a delightsome land, saith The Lord.*** (Malachi 3:12) Wouldn't it be awesome if we were so blessed that other people in our lives noticed? It would be so great that when people talked about us, their conversations behind our backs were about how blessed we really are. That is the promise that God gives. Oh, some will not use the word blessed, for they do not understand it. They may call us "lucky," "successful," or similar words. They may even be jealous of us and treat us as such, but they recognize that we are blessed. And that brings glory to God. I am not suggesting at all that tithing will make us instantly rich. In fact, it may or may not bring us more money, but it will bring us more prosperity. It will bring us more blessings. It will destroy the curses in our lives. We are more apt to receive more finances—because we have been faithful and obedient to The Lord in small things, He can give us more. As we leave this section, let me quote Malachi 3:8-12 from the Jewish Bible.

*Ought man to defraud God? Yet you are defrauding me. And you ask, "How have we been defrauding you?" In tithe and contribution. You are suffering under a curse, yet you go on defrauding me-the whole nation of you. Bring the full tithe into the storehouse, and let there be food in my house, and thus put me to the test-said The Lord of hosts. I will surely open the floodgates of the sky for you and pour down blessings on you; and I will banish the locusts from you, so that they will not destroy the yield of your soil: and your vines in the field shall no longer miscarry-said The Lord of hosts. And all the nations shall account you happy, for you shall be the most desired of lands-said The Lord of hosts.*

Wow! What a benefit for obedience! Think about the curse that would follow us if we do not handle God's money and properties correctly. I would rather be blessed than cursed. We shortchange ourselves when we rob God. And yes, the neglect of the tithe is robbing God. He has given us all that we have, and what he requires is the first 10%. We are just stewards, for it is His.

Jesus made an interesting comment in Luke 17:11: *If therefore ye have not been faithful in the unrighteous mammon, who will commit to trust the true riches?* What are the true riches? Maybe it is the answer to the prayer that we have been praying for so long. Maybe it is the peace that we have been looking for. Maybe it is the ministry that we believe God has called us to. Maybe it is both spiritual and physical. Maybe it is the spouse or children that we desire. No matter what, it is worth more than the money we are holding on to.

## Are We Supposed To Serve Money?

A long time ago, I heard a preacher say something that has always stayed with me. He said; "Money is to serve us; we are not to serve money." That made a lot of sense to me as a teenager and still makes sense to me now. The problem is that most people serve money. And when I say "serve," I literally mean "will do just about anything for money, even in the church."

In Matthew 6:24 Jesus tells us, "No man can serve two masters for either he will hate the one, and love the other; or else he will hold to the one, and despise the other. Ye cannot serve God and mammon (money)." Nowhere does the Bible command us to hoard what we have. That is an anti-Christian mentality. The Bible tells us to give. We have already seen in Malachi that the people were cursed because they hoarded for themselves that which they were supposed to give to God (the tithes and offerings). Hoarding is natural. "Looking out for me" and making sure that I am taken care of first. Mammon (or money) does wonders for the flesh. The more money we have, the more things we can consume upon our lusts and the very thought of giving something up goes against our natural inclinations. See it's natural. However, the natural mind is at war against God. The spiritual mind will give because it's obedient. That natural mind will hoard. And when we hoard our money, we are literally holding on to the one, but neglecting the other (which is the Kingdom of God). Jesus would tell us not to be hoarders, but to "Seek First the Kingdom of God and His Righteousness, then all these things shall be added unto you." (Matthew 6:33) We are still going to be blessed and probably have the desires of our hearts, but instead of robbing God and trying to do it ourselves, God, in turn, does it for us. Our attitude and mentality has just changed. Instead of fulfilling the lust of the flesh, we are now blessed by God because we are working with God instead of trying to do it ourselves. When we are serving God, money is serving us because we are doing it God's way.

## What Is Better Than Stocks?

"Lay not up for yourselves treasures upon earth, where moth and rust doth corrupt, and where thieves break through and steal: but lay up for yourselves treasures in Heaven, where neither moth no rust doth corrupt, and where thieves do not break through nor steal." (Matthew 6:19-20) Jesus was teaching us something here that many may not realize. We can lay up treasures in Heaven. Someone once said that "you can't take it with you." Of course, we can't take it with us, but we can send it before us. We can lay up for ourselves treasure in Heaven. That's better than stocks.

One may say "Pastor, that's where I disagree with you." Let me explain: Do we believe that people will receive rewards in Heaven? Surely, we do; that's biblical. Do we believe those rewards are based upon what we do on earth? How about the martyr? Will he receive a special reward for being a martyr? That's what the Bible declares. Then why would we not receive rewards for our tithes and offerings? That's a sacrifice we are making. Let me be abundantly clear that we cannot buy our way into heaven, nor can we buy a reward. We saw with the rich men giving out of their abundance that Jesus wasn't necessarily impressed even though they gave great riches. What will their reward be in Heaven? I have no idea. However, I can be assured that the poor widow found a way to lay up treasures in heaven, despite the fact that in man's eyes, her gift may have been meager. It's not the amount given; it's the heart-felt reason for giving. Obedience brings rewards. Tithing is obedience. Tithing is thankfulness. Tithing is an act of faith. Giving comes from the heart of love.

Unfortunately, most Christians haven't considered this truth. At the beginning of this story, we talked about the little widow and how she gave her money into the treasure house; she essentially gave to The Lord. She was a wise investor. She placed her money where it was safe. She would not have lost it if the stock market crashed. Someone didn't swindle her out of it. She didn't take her measly coins and fulfill the lust of the flesh. She invested in something greater than herself. She invested it into the Kingdom of God. She wanted to be part of what God was doing. Often Christians have to be persuaded to give an offering and must be taught to give tithes. When they do give, they are looking for it to come back, pressed down, shaken together and running over.

Maybe we are holding on to Proverbs 3:9-10, **"Honour the Lord with thy substance, and with the firstfruits** (tithes) **of all thine increase: So shall thy barns be filled with plenty, and thy presses shall burst out with new wine."** We have talked a lot about the blessing of tithing. We didn't even talk a lot about giving offerings. It does come back to us, and we do honor The Lord with it. It is a sign of our faith in the One who provides our every need. We are literally partnering with God to bring His will to pass. Just as nothing happens without prayer, many things do not happen because Christians won't give. Just as praying is partnering with God, ministry is God using us to bless someone else, so our giving is partnering up with God and ministry. We get to be part of what God is doing. So why don't you look at your bank account right now. Are you doing an effective job partnering up with God? Are you truly worshiping God? Are you obedient to God? Are you trusting God? We have tried to give a logical thought about tithing, but there may be someone who even after reading this booklet that do not believe in tithing-that's ok.

## What do I say to Those Who do not Believe in Tithing?

What do I say to people who do not believe in tithing? Nothing! They have already determined that they won't give. They are cursed with a curse and do not even realize it. Some supposed Bible scholars are teaching that tithing is under the law, and we who teach tithing are legalistic.

We have already proven that tithing came before the law was written. According to George Barna[3], from the market research group that bears his name, in 2007 only 9% of all "born-again" Christians tithed. Are we to believe that only 9% of the church wants to be part of what God is doing? Most of us would probably state that we love God and are trying to be obedient to God, that we thank God for the abundance that he has given to us, and that we take Matthew 6:33 seriously. In fact, every preacher at some point preaches the famous words of Jesus: "Seek ye first the Kingdom of God and His Righteousness and all these things shall be added unto you."

Most of chapter 6 of the book of Matthew instructs us about money. God wants to be first. That sounds as if He still wants the first-fruits, not the excuses. I believe He wants us to have Abel's mentality—not Cain's. After looking at your bank account, what kind of mentality do you have?

It is interesting that we are to seek the Kingdom of God first, and that tithes are the first

[3] https://www.barna.org/barna-update/congregations/41-new-study-shows-trends-in-tithing-and-donating#.VkYc5iRi4zY

10%. Tithes are not just 10%, but the first 10%. That's why some people think that the tithe is a lot of money because they give the last 10% and then have nothing; whereas when they give the first 10%, they still have 90% to use in the way that they wish. I believe very strongly that the tithe is a holy thing—separated unto The Lord. The holy things were not supposed to be like everything else, but were to be set apart for a particular purpose, mainly the purpose of God. When we take something that is designated as holy and contaminate it, it is no longer holy. That first 10% of the first fruits is a holy thing. Before anything else God gives into our care- the Holy Thing. It's not like the rest of our money, for it has been separated out for a particular purpose. We may not see the difference, but God sees that the tithe is for Him.

## Can We Talk?

### *The Missionary*

I had the privilege of having dinner with a missionary not long ago. As we were talking about finances on the mission field, he informed me that he knew of a few missionaries that were not able to continue their call because people quit giving. "They were great missionaries," he explained, "but their finances dried up."

How sad that is! Someone might say, "Well, if God had really called him, God would have made a way." That thought has a lot of validity to it. However, in Isaiah, God lets it be known that He is going to have to destroy a people because no man would stand in the gap or be an intercessor between God and the land. No one would step up. I am suggesting that everything God wants to do is not always accomplished because man doesn't always obey.

Edmund Burke, the Irish Statesmen of the 1700's, has been credited as saying "The only thing necessary for the triumph of evil is for good men to do nothing." I believe that quote is true. We often wonder why God hasn't done something about a particular problem when in fact, it could be that He has, but the person whom God wants to use to answer a particular problem will not co-operate thus instead of the problem(s) being solved, the problem(s) continue or worsen. Because when good men do nothing, evil continues and in fact usually worsens.

"Well, the man should have more faith in God as His provider," someone might say. Maybe, that's true, but let's just say that God did call this individual to quit his job and go over to another country away from the life that he had lived. In essence, God really did call him to be a missionary. The individual still has the responsibility of providing for his family in addition to starting a church from scratch. Wouldn't that be stressful? Now, what happens when he arrives and his American Christian co-laborers who consider praying over a meal, their devotional time, are sitting home in their leather recliners, eating pizza that was just delivered to them, watching a DVD that they rented on a big screen T.V., and have quit supporting him? Do they tell the missionary that he should have more faith that God will provide? What would God do? Did God call every person in the church to be a body and to work as a team to accomplish His goals? In Romans 10:13-15, the Apostle Paul says: "**For whosoever shall call upon The Name of The Lord shall be saved. How then shall they call on him in whom they have not believed? And how shall they believe in him of whom they have**

**not heard? And how shall they hear without a preacher? And how shall they preach, except they be sent?"**

So it is quite possible that God is wanting a missionary to go over to a particular country, for the missionary to see many lives converted, many hungry children-fed, etc. However, because a few good men did not send needed resources to the missionary, lives go unchanged, children continue to die in starvation, etc. In short because a few good men do nothing, evil continues to triumph. This is happening right here and right now. Everyday missionaries are loosing their influence, children are dying of starvation, and the Gospel is not being preached in certain areas because the resources that keeps the missionary there has dried up. Isn't it interesting that it takes someone willing to be sent? Since I believe in the Gospel of Jesus Christ and that it changes lives, I have determined that I will always tithe and give offerings not just because as a Christian I have a mandate to do this but because I want to be part of what God is doing locally and across the world. I want to be an answer to someone's prayer. I want to co-operate with GOD and help bring His desires to pass.

## The Pastor

I started a church about 16 years ago in Columbus Junction, Iowa. My Pastor (Pastor Ronald G. Yohe) sent me there and his church (Faith Chapel in Muscatine) supported us financially. Once a month, Pastor Yohe would send a few of his people over to our community to encourage us. What a strength and an inspiration that was! I labored for over a year and a half without anyone to preach to except my family. I had three people who had tried us out during that time. One visited only once, and the other two stayed with us for less than one month. I could not understand why no one was coming to the church. One Sunday, I was praying behind my pulpit and told God that I must have failed in this community, since He told me to start a church and no one was coming. I told God that day's sermon would be the last message that I would ever preach in this town. I didn't blame God; I didn't blame anyone. It wasn't a threat;

I had just assumed that I either had misunderstood the call to Columbus Junction or that the people just didn't want to hear. After all, Jesus couldn't do some things in some places because the people were not responsive.

Strangely, people would come up to speak to me on the street, thinking that they were encouraging me. They would make statements like, "Oh, you're Pastor McAfee. We have been praying for a church like yours to come into this area. You are an answer to prayer." But they never attended. And because I had determined to go to their city, I was in effect (if they were telling the truth) an answer to their prayer. But they refused to be an answer to mine. They knew that God needed to do something in the city in which they lived, so He put it upon my heart to move from Muscatine, Iowa, which my wife and I were enjoying, to a town 30 minutes away from any decent stores to shop in. He called me away from a 2,400 square foot house to a house of 1,000 square feet. My family and I were dedicated to the call, but the same ones that prayed us into the city were the same ones that refused to join us, let alone support financially the work.

Do I sound bitter? I hope not for I am not bitter in the least. That day that I gave my letter of resignation to God, fourteen Hispanic people visiting from Chicago came into our service. I had fourteen people to sing with and to preach to. I didn't even get a chance to shake their hands, for right after the service, when we said the last "Amen," they came up to the pulpit and shook my hand. They gave joyously to the offering, and they kept me in Columbus Junction. A month later people started attending a few at a time, and now our church is thriving.

One might say "See, God performed a miracle and made a way for you." Absolutely, He did! However, He was not able to use the same Christians who had requested my coming to keep me here. I am convinced that those Christians from Chicago that came on that Sunday morning will receive a great reward for coming and participating in the service. They had no idea that just a few minutes before they came through the door I had prayed the prayer of resignation. They also had no idea that their showing up kept me from leaving.

Even though our church is thriving now, those same people who prayed for a church like ours to come to the community still haven't bothered to attend despite the fact that they feel great that in their minds that we are here because of their prayers.

If they had come, we would have been able to have an impact on our society greater and sooner than we have now. They delayed the hand of God. It is true that they didn't stop the hand of God, but they surely didn't partner with Him, even though it was on their heart to do so. They were obedient to pray and to make the request, but as of this writing they have not been obedient to support us.

## The Traveling Evangelist

I have been on the evangelistic field for a few years. I received a call out of the blue one day to come to New Hartford, NY to preach at a Russian immigrant church. I was surprised by the call because I knew no one in New York. However, I had once preached in a small house church in a small village in Siberia, Russia. A man that was there called his sister who lived in New York and told her that they should consider having me come to their town. I knew nothing about any of this. I didn't even consider that in this small village someone had a sister living in New York.

The pastor called me and asked me to come. I agreed and a date was set. My wife took off work; we loaded our son into the car and drove from Iowa to New York. On the way, we stopped at a few restaurants and even stopped at a motel for the night. When we pulled up to the pastor's house, he informed us that we would be staying and eating with him; we considered it a blessing. We held service for him and God moved most powerfully. We were blessed; they were blessed. It was awesome! As we were leaving to return home, the pastor gave me a check for $500. A person can reason that it is a lot of money for a 2-hour service. I mean, it does break down to making $250 an hour. Not a bad pay. Unless we considered that it took $450 to make the round trip, leaving a profit margin of only $50. That's right, I received a pay of $50 that week. Who can live on $50 a week? The interesting thing was, that I preached to a crowd of

250 people. Breaking down the offering ($500) by the number of people that attended the services (250 people) that would be the equivalent of every person giving $2.00 as an offering. My point is that often we do not consider that when we have special guest speakers, they, too, have bills to pay, families to feed, finances to reach next location, and a household to support.

Now I must say that God made up the difference because of our obedience, and we lacked nothing. Most evangelists could tell you about financial miracles that God has performed. But there are others who had to leave the evangelistic field; there are missionaries who had to leave the field; and there are pastors who have left the pastoral field because they ran out of money. Many of these pastors, evangelists and missionaries who have had to abandon their pastoral fields, feel like failures. They are not failures. They answered the call of God. But those who refused to support are the failures. Remember, the only thing necessary for the triumph of evil is for good men to do nothing. We live in an evil world, and it is getting more evil all the time. One reason is that people that God has called into the missionary, pastoral and evangelistic field can not continue because Christians have stopped giving.

I know of a missionary to Kazakhstan whose funds from supporters back in the States dried up. Because he believed God, he continued to live and minister, build churches, and start schools etc... in Kazakhstan. He lived off his credit card for over 2 years. At the end of 2 years, he came back home on leave and was forced to get a job to pay off his credit card. God was gracious to him, and he was able to pay it off, but not without living in a rundown trailer in his in-laws' yard and working at a pizza joint for 3 years. He lost 3 years of working his mission because of a lack of funds. Someone dropped the ball, and it wasn't God or the missionary.

Let me re-iterate what George Barna's study found; only 9% of "Born-again" Christians tithe. From the pastors that I have talked with, they would say that only about 22% of their congregation gives finances on a regular basis to their church. That's probably why the church can't keep a pastor, why they can't bring in a youth pastor, why they can't build a decent parking lot, why they aren't feeding the poor, why they can't evangelize appropriately, why they aren't causing the church to grow—the list of what a church can't afford to do is endless. What would The Red Cross do if they did not have supporters? NOTHING. Conversely, what could the church do if people who believed in God would have the same concept of worship, giving and faith as Abel or the widow that we previously mentioned? What could the church accomplish if instead of 22% of the church attendees just giving, that they actually tithed? What if 50% of the church attendees tithed, or 75% tithed or 100% tithed? We could probably do everything that God has commanded us to do: feed the poor, clothe the naked, evangelize, support missions, etc.

## <u>I Would Like To Give, But I Just Don't Have Much Money</u>

I have often heard people say what they would do if they had a lot of money. Most of them say that they would give, give, and give. People have said "I wish I had money to give." Some say, "My little bit would not influence anyone nor would it be much of a contribution."

First, we have already established that the tithe is always the first 10%, so if you have anything, then you automatically have the first 10%.

Secondly, if we go back to our text about the widow giving 2/5ths of a penny. She didn't influence anyone-except Jesus. And isn't Jesus the only one that we should be influencing anyway. Jesus was excited about the 2/5ths of a cent and was more impressed with her small gift than all the other much larger gifts.

Thirdly, how can we determine how much contribution our gift will make on somebody or some project? In John 6:1-14 we see about 5,000 men sitting listening to Jesus. Jesus says to one of the disciples, "Where can we buy bread to feed the people?" His disciple said, "Jesus, we can't buy enough bread to sufficiently feed this many." Another of Jesus disciples brings to Jesus a boy, that had five loaves of bread and two fishes, but then says, "But what are they among so many?"[4] That is a very interesting question: how could the boy's small gift make any contribution to feeding and meeting the need of such a multitude of

---

[4]  John 6:9b

people? But once given into the hand of Jesus, it not only sufficiently met the need, but also produced 12 baskets left over. Jesus can make even the smallest of our gifts sufficient enough to make an impact for The Kingdom of God, but we have to be willing to give and not to withhold.

## Should We Give As We Are Led?

I once read that tithing was outdated and that we needed to start "giving as The Spirit leads." First, I think that we have established that tithing is not outdated. But it is true that we need to give as The Spirit leads, but this is another concept. We spend the majority of our time talking about tithing because that is the foundation of church finances. **Bring ye all tithe into the storehouse, that there may be meat in mine house** (Malachi 3:10a) Giving as The Spirit leads sounds spiritual, but often it is based upon what we deem to be important or what we feel like we can or want to give. This is not the argument for tithing. This is the argument for offerings. We tithe because The Spirit has already told us to in The Word. The Spirit will never tell you to do something that is unbiblical. And withholding our tithe from the church is unbiblical. However, after giving the tithe, it is quite possible and probable that there are times when The Holy Spirit will speak to you about giving to someone, some mission, or some need that is beyond the tithe. That is proper theology of "giving as the Spirit leads."

## A Word to Preachers

1. Quit begging for money! Teach tithing; give opportunities for the people to worship The Lord in giving of their substance. But quit begging. We are children of The Most High, The King of kings. I didn't beg in the world, and I surely am not going to beg in The Kingdom. I told my church that I would never tell them about a light bill and never tell them about the needs of the church in the way of finances. I would close the church down before having to do that. If everyone walks in obedience, we won't have a financial problem—at least not one that God wouldn't be willing to get us out of.

2. Receive tithes and offerings by faith. We all know that it takes money to operate ministry. Though ministry is expensive, God has not called us to worry about the money. Of course, we have to be good stewards and we cannot amass debts that we can't pay for. But we have to realize that this is ultimately God's ministry, and it is His responsibility to bring in the cash.

3. Tithe! I have met too many preachers who do not tithe. They will receive the tithe of others, but they do not tithe themselves. Somehow they have justified that they are above tithing. If tithing is an act of thanksgiving, if it is an act of faith, if it is an act of worship, if it is an act of obedience, then how can anyone be above tithing? We must all be people who tithe; in fact, the preacher should be the example. A preacher should never be a thief. I believe it is hypocritical for ministers to preach while robbing God.

4. As a pastor, if you are going to bring someone in to speak, then you should treat them graciously in the aspect of finances.

There are a variety of church sizes, and a small church can't be required to do what an average size or a large church can do. But all should try and treat the guest graciously in the aspect of finances. A good rule of thumb is to provide for your guest's room and lodging. Also, if it is a full time evangelist, missionary, or someone whose full-time job is to travel in ministry, you should attempt to pay their honorarium the equivalent of a work week for the average attender of your church. In other words if your average attender makes $500 a week, that is what you should attempt to pay your guest. If your average attender makes $1,000 a week, that should be what you attempt to pay your guest. Should my guest be paid a full week salary for speaking for a couple of hours? Absolutely, that is his full time job, and he has expenses just as everyone else does.

# A Final Word

1) We should be people who tithe. Not only should we tithe, we should be generous in giving. People might excuse themselves because they do not feel as if they have enough to give. That didn't keep the widow from giving. She had very little, yet she gave to God anyway.

2) I believe that the measure that we give is the measure that we will receive; actually we receive more than we give because if God can trust us with little, He can trust us with much. I believe that is the number one reason why many do not have more—they can't be trusted with it.

3) Ministry takes money. Just as a family cannot have certain things because they lack the finances, so, too, the church cannot have certain things and more importantly, can't do certain things because of a lack in finances. Would we like to have a better parking lot at the church? It takes money. Does the building need to look better, or do the seats need to be more comfortable? It takes money. Would you rather have a better children's ministry? It takes money. Ministry does take money. Missions take money. Growth and expansion takes money. Feeding the poor takes money.

4) I hate the fact that most churches do fund-raisers outside the church. As a youth leader, I decided to take our teens to Six Flags Great America. In order to raise funds, our teens went door-to-door selling fire extinguishers and first aid kits. Our teens were humiliated as door after door was slammed in their faces. I thought to myself, "Why should the church, which is blessed by God and called by God, somehow

believe that the non-believers should pay for the Church of God?" I approached the pastor that I was working for (Pastor Ron Yohe) and told him what I had observed. He instructed me to throw out the fund raising plan and to take the teens to Six Flags. I have never again asked non-believers to pay for something the church wanted or needed to do. I am a firm believer that with everyone doing his or her part, the church will be self-sustaining. It is true that some can't give much, but others can give more. It equals out. Then the church will have enough to support the local work of God.

# Conclusion

M ost of us know that The Bible is considered a mirror. It doesn't play favorites. The Bible shows us our hearts. It shows us what we are doing well, what we are doing badly, what we are neglecting to do, how we can improve, what God thinks of us. The Bible is a mirror for it shows no favorites and it shows us who we really are. The other mirror is our checkbook.

*"For where your treasure is, there will your heart be also."* Matthew 6:21

Jesus himself expressed that we can see our own heart by looking at our checkbook or debit card receipts. A mirror doesn't lie as we have already determined. It shows accurately the image that is before it. One's checkbook doesn't lie either. It shows accurately what is of value to its owner. That's one of the biggest arguments that I would have for people who believe that they must give "as The Spirit directs" and not a tithe. My argument would be for them to look at their checkbook, and determine what percentage of their finances went to satisfy the flesh (restaurants, movies, and entertainment) compared to what percentage went to the work of The Lord. If Jesus was correct that our hearts are wherever we put our money, then maybe we need to put God first (tithes, first-fruits) and all these things will be added unto us. In other words we don't lose out. Truly it is more blessed to give than to receive.

I am concerned with the world, and more specifically about America. If Jesus is right and where our treasure is reflects our heart, and George Barna is right that only 9% of people who claim to be born again Christians tithe, and only 22% give anything to the church, that really shows a major spiritual problem that needs to be repented of. Has the American church fallen into a curse like the Israelites that Malachi preached to? And more importantly, what about us as individuals? What does the mirror in our lives say about our spiritual condition? Do we truly want a spiritual revival? How can it happen if our churches, evangelists, missionaries are financially anemic? Let's just remember that the rich young ruler in Matthew 19: 15-24 even though he spoke to Jesus about eternal life, even though he was interested in eternal life, even though he was very interested in a change of life, he still walked away from Jesus sorrowful, for he really got to see himself in the mirror for who he was. He loved money more than God. He was more interested in money than in God.

## Conclusion

1. Tithing was before The Law. Thus it is not legalistic to tithe.
2. God owns everything; we are just entrusted with it.
3. Being good stewards entails spending God's money the way He wants it spent.
4. There are many benefits to tithing.
5. Tithing is being obedient.

6. Tithing shows our gratitude.
7. Tithing is worship.
8. Tithing is a practical way of walking in faith.
9. Tithing allows me to partner with God to bring His will to pass.

Remember:

## *"For where your treasure is, there will your heart be also."* Matthew 6:21

## Bio of Mrs. Sandra Martin:

I would like to consider myself a "Christian educator in the public school system." I was born 1946 in central Iowa, was educated in a small rural high school in Colo, Iowa, and received my BA degree in secondary English education from the University of Northern Iowa. I taught English for 5 years at Woodward-Granger High School, just 20 miles northwest of Des Moines, then moved to Columbus Junction where I taught English for 36 years. My husband of 45 years, my son, my two daughters, and my 8 grandchildren are the joy of my life.

## Bio of Michael McAfee:

Michael was saved at the age of 14 and started preaching when he was 16. He traveled as an Evangelist from 1991 until 1994 when he came on staff at Faith Chapel in Muscatine, serving under Pastor Ronald G. Yohe's leadership. While accountable to the Senior Pastor, he worked out of Faith Chapel as an Evangelist but also worked with his Pastor on outreaches. In 1999, Faith Chapel sent Michael to Columbus Junction to church plant. Michael is the founder and Senior Pastor of Victory Christian Center of Columbus Junction and is the founder and President of One Touch Ministry (his evangelistic Ministry). Michael has been married to his wife, Jolene for 23 years and together they have two children: Matthew (and his wife Molly) and Morgan.

# BIBLIOGRAPHY

1. Barna.org
2. All scripture is taken from King James Bible unless stated differently
3. The Jewish Study Bible, Oxford University Press New York, New York 2004
4. Snow White & The Seven Dwarfs, Treasure Box of Children's Stories, platt & Munk Co. 1922
   a. I told the story from Memory so Not exactly for sure how to put that down, if needed.
5. Dickens, Charles. A Christmas Carol: A Ghost Story of Christmas. London: Chapman & Hall 1843
6. The Christmas Carol, from the story written by Charles Dickens,
   a. Directed by Edwin L. Marin
   b. Produced by Joseph L. Mankiewicz
   c. Screen Play written by Hugo Butler
   d. Released Dec. 16,1938